BRITISH RAILWAYS

PAST and PRESENT

No 36

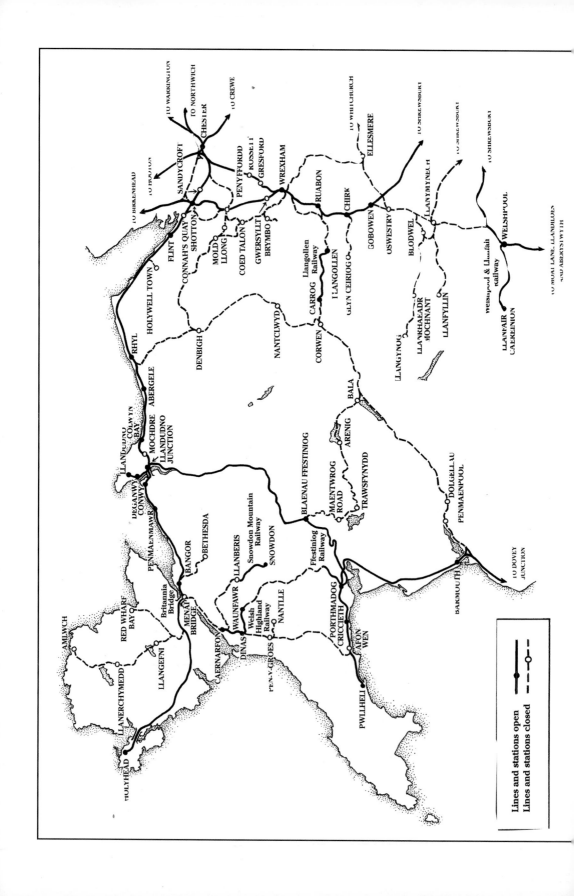

BRITISH RAILWAYS

PAST and PRESENT

No 36

North Wales

Paul Shannon & John Hillmer

Past and
Present

Past & Present Publishing Ltd

© Paul Shannon & John Hillmer 2001

First published in 2001

British Library Cataloguing in Publication Data

A catalogue record for this book is available from the British Library.

ISBN 1 85895 163 1

Past & Present Publishing Ltd
The Trundle
Ringstead Road
Great Addington
Kettering
Northants
NN14 4BW

Tel/Fax: 01536 330588
email: sales@nostalgiacollection.com
website: www.nostalgiacollection.com

Map drawn by Christina Siviter

Printed and bound in Great Britain

BIBLIOGRAPHY

Complete British Railways Maps & Gazetteer 1830-1981 *by C. J. Wignall (OPC)*

Directory of Railway Stations *by R. V. J. Butt (Patrick Stephens Ltd)*

Forgotten Railways: North & Mid Wales *by Rex Christiansen (David & Charles)*

Handbook of Steam Motive Power Depots *by Paul Smith (Platform 5)*

Historical Survey of the Chester-Holyhead Railway *by Anderson & Fox (OPC)*

A Regional History of the Railways of Great Britain: Volume 11, North & Mid Wales *by Peter E. Baughan (David & Charles)*

Scenes From The Past: Railways of North Wales series *by W. G. Rear/N. Jones/M. F. Williams (Foxline)*

CONTENTS

LLANDUDNO JUNCTION (Cyffordd Llandudno): During the period when Class 33s were working regularly on the North Wales coast line, No 33032 rounds the curve into Llandudno Junction with the 1740 from Llandudno to Crewe on 19 September 1986. In 1985 Crewe station underwent considerable alteration and there was a period when the Holyhead-Cardiff service went via Wrexham (the loco 'running round' at Chester), which took Class 33s into Wrexham for a period. This more direct route is being used again from the Summer timetable of 2000 with the new Cardiff-Holyhead service, with Llandudno being included for the first time.

On the left in the 'past' picture is the estuary of the River Conwy, which appears to have disappeared in our new photograph! Not so. What has happened is that a tunnel has been built under the estuary to accommodate the upgraded A55 Expressway – the tunnel entrance can be seen just left of centre – and a great deal of landscaping was necessary. In the 'present' picture Class 158 No 158755 forms the 1440 from 'The Queen of Resorts' to Manchester Piccadilly on 2 July 1999. *Gavin Morrison/JCH*

BRITANNIA BRIDGE: Ex-LMS 'Black Five' 4-6-0 No 44860 comes out of the up tube at the eastern end of the bridge across the Menai Strait on a summer's day in 1962. Stephenson's Tubular Bridge celebrated its 150th anniversary on 25 March 2000, having survived a disastrous fire in 1970 that closed it for more than 18 months and isolated Anglesey 'railwise' from the mainland.

A road deck, which dominates the 'present' picture taken on 16 March 2000, was added in the late 1970s, but one of the lions can still be seen on the right-hand side of the bridge. The line over the bridge is now only single track. *E. N. Kneale/JCH*

INTRODUCTION

Croeso! Welcome to North Wales, a region where railway history blends with stunning scenery to produce some fascinating 'past and present' comparisons. A few traces still remain today of some of the earliest industrial railways that brought slate and minerals down from the hills. However, many long-closed lines, stations and terminals have either been redeveloped beyond recognition or have completely returned to nature. Other pairs of pictures have a more positive story to tell, with new or improved stations and modern rolling-stock providing evidence of recent and ongoing investment. But pictures of the last-mentioned type are a minority!

It is a sobering thought that the decline of railways in North Wales started in the 1930s, barely half a century after the peak years of 'railway mania'. First came the withdrawal of little-used passenger services to Red Wharf Bay, Glynceiriog and Dyserth, followed in the 1950s by Llangynog and Holywell Town. But it was in the 1960s that Dr Beeching's 'axe' brought the most dramatic decline, with the closure of branches to Amlwch, Bethesda, Llanberis and Llanfyllin, and of through routes from Caernarfon to Afon Wen, Ruabon to Morfa Mawddach, Bala to Blaenau Ffestiniog, Rhyl to Corwen and Denbigh to Corwen. The stub from Bangor to Caernarfon just lasted into 1970. Today's skeletal network resulting from these closures radiates mainly from the English centres of Shrewsbury and Chester. We make no apologies for including in this Welsh volume several shots of Chester, always considered to be a railway gateway to North Wales. Likewise, the inclusion of Oswestry seems logical.

North Wales passenger operations in the last few years have witnessed a welcome revival, thanks largely to the efforts of the privatised franchise-holders. The region has seen fewer station re-openings than many parts of Britain – Conwy being the most recent example in 1987 – but overall passenger numbers are growing, and, on the North Wales coast line at least, train frequencies are increasing. Unfortunately from the enthusiast's point of view the modernisation of the railway infrastructure, enabling trains to run more efficiently, has meant the loss of many traditional railway features such as signal boxes, gantries and intricate yard and siding layouts. We have included several comparisons where the 'past' picture was taken less than 20 years ago but belongs to a different railway era from the 'present' one.

The change from steam to diesel traction in the 1960s is rightly seen as a watershed in British railway history. The smaller, more efficient diesel fleet needed fewer maintenance facilities, and by the end of the 1970s the only servicing locations in North Wales were Holyhead, Llandudno Junction and, tenuously, Croes Newydd. By the late 1990s only Holyhead remained active as a fuelling point, and the units used in North Wales were supplied mainly from Newton Heath (Manchester), Longsight (Manchester) and Tyseley (Birmingham) depots. As for locomotive haulage, this held out for longer in North Wales than in most parts of the country, with Classes 37 and 47 still in use by First North Western and Virgin West Coast respectively in the first year of the new millennium.

The preservation movement has been responsible for bringing trains back to a number of North Wales lines in the last few decades. We have included a couple of scenes from the Llangollen Railway, which now arguably enjoys greater prosperity than it did in its latter years as part of the through route from Wrexham to the coast. Hopes are high that the Amlwch branch will be re-activated as a heritage railway. The narrow-gauge Ffestiniog Railway provides a successful transport link between Blaenau Ffestiniog and Porthmadog, as well as bringing pleasure to thousands of visitors in the summer months. Another significant route will be opened up when the Welsh Highland Railway is re-instated between Caernarfon and Porthmadog.

The carriage of freight by rail deserves special mention in a book such as this. Often railway photographers paid little attention to goods trains in the 1950s and 1960s, mainly because they were so commonplace. The pattern of closures up to the Beeching period generally saw freight outlive passenger workings for a few years. However, from the 1970s onwards that pattern was reversed, with freight facilities being progressively withdrawn from the now passenger-orientated network. The all-stations pick-up goods train declined sharply up to the 1960s and effectively ceased to exist in the 1970s. The only surviving freight-only lines by the 1970s were those that had a major source of trainload business such as the ARC quarry at Blodwel and Associated Octel at Amlwch. Today, even those lines have lost their traffic, and in the whole of North Wales there is not a single freight-only line. On the North Wales coast line, the end of Irish container traffic was a severe blow, accompanied by the loss of smaller flows such as cement to Bangor and oil to Llandudno Junction. But the freight picture is not entirely negative. At the time of writing Penmaenmawr quarry remains an important source of ballast, the Kronospan factory at Chirk is taking in unprecedented volumes of timber, and steel for export to Ireland is being railed to Mostyn Docks.

We view the future of the North Wales railway network with some optimism. It is likely that present trends in passenger operations will continue, with Class 175 'Coradia' DMUs providing a fillip for passengers on the coast line and with the prospect of new through services such as that between Holyhead and Cardiff introduced by Wales & West in 2000. The outlook for freight is perhaps less certain – the Irish container traffic in particular seems to be a lost cause – but, with EWS and other freight operators campaigning hard to win new business and to enlist political support, there may yet be some interesting revivals.

Our grateful thanks go to all the photographers who allowed us to use their pictures, without which the book would not have been possible. Special mention must go to Michael Mensing, Gavin Morrison and Norman Kneale, and to Bryan Wilson for his help with dates and other historical details.

John Hillmer, Wilmslow
Paul Shannon, Chester

10

Anglesey

HOLYHEAD (Caergybi) (1): Before the new station facilities were built in the late 1980s, it was possible to have a close-up sight of the Irish ferry ships. In the 'past' photograph, taken on 7 July 1985, there is a clear view of the *St Columba*, while in the foreground Class 08 No 08613 shunts stock.

With the new buildings, the station was also given a footbridge leading into the town. On 16 March 2000 Class 37 No 37401 is 'running round' its train, having brought in the 1007 from Birmingham New Street. After the introduction of the new Class 175 'Coradia' units, it seems likely that the only loco-hauled trains will be some of the Euston services. *Both JCH*

of the harbour. There were daily Freightliner services to Trafford Park (Manchester), Lawley Street (Birmingham) and Willesden/Stratford in London, as well as a fourth train to Basford Hall, Crewe, for connections with other trunk services. On 15 May 1982 Class 40 No 40060 is departing with a consist of empty 'flats'. Later these trains were all diagrammed for Class 47s.

When the Port of Holyhead lost the container business, the site was totally transformed. The tracks and overhead cranes have all disappeared and been replaced by a modern departure area for all forms of road transport *en route* to Ireland, seen in the 'present' picture dated 1 May 1998. Class 37 No 37422 has 'run-round' having arrived with the 1007 from Birmingham New Street. *Both JCH*

HOLYHEAD (Caergybi) (3). A great deal has happened in the 13 years since the "past" photograph was taken on 8 July 1965, as Class 47, No 47532 comes "off shed" and prepares to back down on to its coaches waiting in the station. The four-road brick-built loco-shed was closed to steam in 1966, although it continued in diesel use well into the 1980s. It was subsequently demolished and replaced by a small modern structure with limited facilities.

Considerable track rationalisation has taken place and the scene on 3 March 2000 shows one of devastation. The A5 road is in the process of considerable upgrading, but beyond the works it can be seen that the signal box still stands and some semaphore signals continue in use. The town's skyline has changed, including the disappearance of a church, but there are several buildings that are still recognisable. *Both JCH*

13

LLANGEFNI: In this undated overall view of the station, looking south towards Gaerwen, where the branch joine[
the main line between Bangor and Holyhead, there is a train in the station platform and the yard contains lime
washed cattle wagons. The view undoubtedly dates from before the 1923 Grouping – note the horse-drawn
vehicle coming down the station approach. At its peak there were two and occasionally three goods trains each
day, mainly for livestock, running into the yard, which is now a car park.

In the new picture, taken on 27 February 2000 from the closest point to where the original was taken, th[
station building is in the foreground, now in private ownership, but the platform has gone. Long after th[
cessation of passenger traffic there was a regular chemicals train to Associated Octel at Amlwch, but eventuall[
this was transferred by the company to road transport. Hopefully the line will be brought back to life with it
likely purchase by Anglesey Council. *Len's of Sutton/JCH*

14

LLANERCHYMEDD: This other intermediate station on the Amlwch branch was opened in 1866. Later to be absorbed into the LNWR, then the LMS and finally British Railways, it was closed just two years short of celebrating its centenary. The 'past' shot, looking south probably not long before closure, shows a clean and tidy station, but when the 'present' photograph was taken on 17 February 2000, the site was a desolate and deteriorating scene, but there is hope for the future as Anglesey Council has plans to purchase the line and re-open it to passenger traffic again. *Len's of Sutton/JCH*

Gwynedd coast and branches

CAERNARFON (1): During the 1950s the station underwent a number of alterations, including the erection of a new waiting shelter on the 'island' platform and the removal of the covering to the footbridge that connected the platforms. In the 1960s BR Class '4' No 75027, with the blower on and safety-valves lifting, waits to depart with the 7.45am SO Pwllheli to Manchester Exchange service.

Passenger services ended in 1970, but the line remained open until 1972, in use as a temporary Freightliner terminal during the period when the Britannia Bridge was being re-built. Today the site is covered by a supermarket and car park, and only the church spire remains to connect the two pictures, as seen in the 'present' shot taken on 30 May 2000. *E. N. Kneale/JCH*

CAERNARFON (2): This view of the approach road to the station, looking north, is undated, but is after 1911 (when the booking hall and canopy were added to the original station); as only horse-drawn traffic can be seen, it was perhaps taken during the First World War. Bangor Road is on the right. Originally opened by the Bangor & Carnarvon Railway in 1852 as 'Carnarvon', it was subsequently re-named 'Caernarvon' by the LMS in 1926. It was an important station on the through line from Bangor to Afon Wen, giving rail connections to Pwllheli or south to Barmouth and beyond, as well as being the junction station for Llanberis. Passenger services survived until 1970.

Today the site is occupied by a supermarket and car park, as seen in the 'present' picture taken on 10 November 1999. Although the town is cut off from the main railway system, the Welsh Highland Railway now runs from Caernarfon to Waunfawr and work is proceeding to run right through to Porthmadog eventually. *Len's of Sutton/JCH*

LLANBERIS: The branch to Llanberis left the Menai Bridge to Afon Wen line a few miles south of Caernarfon. Opened by the LNWR on 1 July 1869, the 8-mile line commenced with five trains each way daily. Tourist traffic increased after the opening of the Snowdon Mountain Railway, but not enough to make an all-year round service viable, and scheduled passenger services were withdrawn in 1930. However, the line remained open for excursion traffic until 1962. The photograph shows the last freight service on 3 September 1964, hauled tender first by ex-LMS Class '5' No 44711.

With the wonderful mountain scenery in the background it is not difficult to find the site of the old station, which is now a Craft Centre, as seen in the 'present' picture taken on 30 May 2000 at 7.45 on a glorious sunny morning! *E. N. Kneale/JCH*

DINAS is a few miles south of Caernarfon on the line to Afon Wen. Its name was originally Dinas Junction when it was an interchange with the North Wales Narrow Gauge Railway, but it was changed to 'Dinas (Caerns)' by the LMS in 1938, following the cessation of the narrow gauge in 1936. Passenger services were withdrawn in 1951, but the line remained open until 1964. When the Welsh Highland was running from Dinas to Porthmadog, the nameboard on the standard-gauge platform proclaimed 'Change here for Snowdon, Beddgelert, Portmadoc & Blaenau Ffestiniog'. The 'past' photograph shows a Derby 'Lightweight' unit running through with a Bangor-Pwllheli local on 26 April 1963.

The Millennium Commission-backed project to restore a narrow-gauge railway from Caernarfon to Porthmadog was opened to Dinas in 1997 by the Welsh Highland and Ffestiniog Railways, and, following a Public Enquiry, the continuation is well in progress and reached Waunfawr in August 2000. The 'present' picture was taken on 30 May 2000 and shows that the narrow gauge track has replaced the standard gauge. The 1300 from Caernarfon is arriving with Beyer Peacock No 143 at the head. *Welsh Railways Research Circle, Stratton Collection/JCH*

PEN-Y-GROES: This carefully posed picture, dating back to *circa* 1885 with an LNWR 0-6-0 commandeered for the occasion, includes a mixture of station staff, permanent way men and passengers, formally dressed and not a bare head to be seen. The imposing station building includes accommodation for the Station Master, but the canopy does not appear to offer much protection when crossing the platform to reach a train. A few miles south of Caernarfon, this was the junction for the Nantlle branch. The station survived until closure in 1964, the final year for the line to Afon Wen.

The trackbed was ultimately turned into a footpath and cycleway, but change is again afoot as it is about to become the village bypass. The road bridge survives and what appears to be part of one of the platforms, but little else, as seen on 30 May 2000. *By permission of the National Library of Wales, John Thomas Collection/JCH*

NANTLLE: Originally a tram road for the conveyance of copper and slate to Pen-y-Groes, it was not until the early 1870s that the branch was converted to standard gauge and a single-platform station with goods shed and turntable was erected at Talysarn, but known as Nantlle. The short branch from Pen-y-Groes was only 1⅜th of a mile, single track and opened to passengers in October 1872, operated by the LNWR. The photograph, taken around 1885, shows the interchange sidings with narrow-gauge slate wagons, and an LNWR 0-6-2T with a short train of four-wheel stock.

The branch had a chequered history with the station closing and re-opening on several occasions, until finally complete closure came on 2 December 1963. Today the area is a car park and children's playground, as seen in the 'present' photograph taken on 30 May 2000. *By permission of the National Library of Wales, John Thomas Collection/JCH*

PWLLHELI (1): The terminus of the Cambrian from Dovey Junction, the existing station was the second to be built; the first was well to the east, whereas the replacement was much closer to the town centre and was opened in 1909. The 'past' picture, taken in the early 1960s, shows Collett 0-6-0 No 2236 standing on one side of the platform with a mixed goods. The tender is piled high with coal and one wonders where she is off to!

The station was subsequently reduced to a single platform face to allow for the development of a supermarket. On 30 May 2000 Class 156 No 156407 is ready to leave for Machynlleth with the 1137 service. In the Summer timetable of 2000, on weekdays there are six down trains and (curiously) seven in the up direction. On Saturdays there are seven each way, and just three on Sundays. There are basic facilities at Pwllheli for the overnight stabling of units. *E. N. Kneale (2)/JCH*

PWLLHELI (2): In the early 1960s, BR Standard 2-6-2T No 82031 is seen approaching Pwllheli with the 'Cambrian Coast Express' portion. On the right is the goods yard where the BR locomotive shed was also situated; the depot water column can be seen in the background.

On 30 May 2000, other than the curve in the track, there is nothing to link the two pictures; the line here has been singled and the crossing now has automatically controlled barriers. The Cambrian route is operated by Central Trains and all services are worked by DMUs with a home base of Tyseley in Birmingham, although light maintenance is carried out at Machynlleth depot. There are no signals and the line is controlled from Machynlleth signal box, by the Radio Electronic Block System (RETB). *E. N. Kneale/JCH*

25

PWLLHELI (3): The BR shed was the third (and final) one, opened in 1959 following the closure of the Cambrian/GWR facility. Built fairly close by, it was a modern structure with two dead-end roads, and was a sub-shed to Machynlleth (89C); it closed in 1966. BR Standard 2-6-2T No 82000 is seen here with a Collett 0-6-0 behind it.

The shed building has survived, with modifications, in the middle of an industrial park and now contains boats! Seen on 30 May 2000, it is remarkable that at one side of the shed there remains a short length of track with an ashpit! *E. N. Kneale/JCH*

BUTLINS PENYCHAIN: A few miles east of Pwllheli a station was opened in 1933 as 'Penychain Halt'; it was renamed 'Penychain' in 1947, and finally had the 'Butlins' prefix added. After the Second World War there was heavy traffic to the Pwllheli Holiday Camp, and a 'Butlins Special' even ran from South Wales. However, as the use of the private car and coach travel increased, fewer holidaymakers travelled by train. On 6 July 1963 an unidentified 2-6-4T is seen in the station.

There have been some alterations to the station building, but it is maintained in very good condition and a most intricate series of ramps has been built to give easy access for passengers. The 'present' picture was taken on 30 May 2000. *Peter Rose/JCH*

CRICCIETH station was opened in 1867 by the Aberystwyth & Welch (sic) Coast Railway, later to be amalgamated with the Cambrian when the line to Pwllheli commenced operation. Rail traffic grew as the area became increasingly popular with tourists. Seen on 6 July 1963, BR Standard 2-6-2T No 82034 moves away towards Barmouth.

Today the goods shed has gone, the line has been singled and only the up platform is in use. Class 156 'Super Sprinter' No 156416 leaves with the 0942 Central Trains service from Pwllheli to Machynlleth on 30 May 2000. *Peter Rose/JCH*

Menai Bridge to Bangor

MENAI BRIDGE: BR '2MT' 2-6-0 No 78059 shunts the station yard in the 1950s. Opened in 1858 by the Chester & Holyhead Railway, the station lasted until 1966. The line to Caernarfon left the main line to Holyhead at the east end of the station, and can be glimpsed on the extreme left.

Apart from the Bangor-Holyhead track itself, virtually everything else has been swept away and replaced by a small industrial estate, as seen in March 2000. However, there is one common feature: just to the left of the goods shed, above the van, can be seen a chimney that survives in the 'present' picture, to the left of the telegraph pole. *Both E. N. Kneale*

BANGOR (1): Prior to the opening of the Britannia Bridge, Bangor was the terminus of the Chester & Holyhead Railway, having been opened in 1848. The original buildings were designed by Francis Thompson, but were subsequently added to. Although the date of the 'past' picture is unknown, the building is on the up side and close examination discloses a number of interesting features. There are several references to the London & North Western Railway, the horse-drawn bus is marked 'British Hotel', which perhaps implies courtesy transport to that establishment, there are a large number of station staff on view (a remarkable contrast with today), and an advertisement for the *Manchester Evening Chronicle* suggests either a wide distribution of that paper or considerable passenger traffic between the two cities.

In the early 1920s the station was expanded, turning the up platform into an 'island'. On 2 July 1999 the 'present' picture clearly shows where this up loop went, but also the fact that it has been subsequently removed!
Len's of Sutton/JCH

BANGOR (2): Taken from Bangor Mountain in 1963, looking west, this wonderful view of the station shows how it was expanded, with the original Francis Thompson building incorporated into the east end of the up 'island' platform on the right. Although the demise of steam was approaching, the engine shed shows plenty of activity and a BR Ivatt 2-6-2T stands in the bay platform (known locally as the 'Bethesda Bay') just to the right of Bangor No 1 signal box.

In the 'present' shot, taken on 2 July 1999, cars can be seen where the up platform loop once was, the canopy on the down platform has been cut back, and although the tree growth obscures the position, Bangor No 1 box has long gone. Bangor No 2 box can, however, still be seen at the far end above the footbridge. The loco shed still stands, but is now in commercial use, and although it appears that the down loop is still there, it is in fact a long siding. An unidentified Class 37 stands at the head of the 1048 Holyhead to Birmingham New Street train. *E. N. Kneale/JCH*

PENMAENMAWR: For many years the local quarry has produced ballast for railway use. In the first picture, taken on 4 May 1983, Class 40 No 40150 (with special headboard commemorating the Class's Silver Jubilee Year), stands at the head of a (mainly) empty ballast train. The second picture shows the modernisation of the conveyor system bringing the stone for loading at the sidings, which contain four fully loaded ballast trains with Class 47 No 47204 at the head of one of them, on 2 May 1985.

Due to the building of the A55 Expressway, the sidings had to undergo some alterations, being reduced to four roads, as seen in the third picture taken on 13 January 2000. Although virtually empty on this occasion, the quarry continues to supply ballast, and in the summer of 2000 there was usually a daily train to Crewe Basford Hall. *Gavin Morrison/JCH (2)*

CONWY: On 21 April 1983 Class 40 No 40170 passes through the site of the old station with a Freightliner service from Trafford Park, Manchester, to Holyhead. The station closed in 1966, and following the loss of the Irish container traffic at the Port of Holyhead, Freightliners are no longer to be seen on the line, although there remains the possibility that one day the traffic may re-commence.

As can be seen in the 'present' picture, taken on 28 March 2000, a new station has been built and was opened in 1987. A market is now held in the station yard and the Erskine Hotel is undergoing a 'facelift'. EWS-liveried Class 37 No 37421 heads the 1251 Holyhead to Crewe service, one of the dying breed of locomotive-hauled trains that was due to be ousted by Class 175 units during 2000. *Gavin Morrison/JCH*

37

Llandudno and Llandudno Junction

LLANDUDNO: The first station was opened by the Chester & Holyhead Railway in 1858, and the existing ex-LNWR terminus dates back to 1892. The date of our 'past' picture is reckoned to be around 1938 and the line of cabs certainly indicates much busier times than now. On the right stands an LNWR 'Cauliflower', probably No 8385, which was allocated to Llandudno Junction shed, with a train for Blaenau Ffestiniog.

Subsequently the overall roof has been greatly cut back, leaving barely cover for even one coach. Apart from the central carriageway, only the clock and the outline of the roofs connect the two pictures. The 'present' picture was taken on 2 July 1999 and shows two-car Class 158 DMU No 158758 (based at Manchester Newton Heath depot) ready to depart at 1336 for Manchester Piccadilly. Other than any specials, normally only DMUs use the station these days. Apart from local destinations, most services go to Crewe or Manchester, but with the start of the Summer 2000 timetable a Cardiff to Holyhead train (and return) travels up and down the branch to serve Llandudno. *Len's of Sutton/JCH*

DEGANWY: On 31 March 1963 BR 'Britannia' Class 4-6-2 No 70019 *Lightning* heads the 4.05pm Llandudno-Birmingham New Street service. Although in the early Summer of 2000 there is one loco-hauled service on the branch from Manchester Piccadilly to Llandudno, this will cease once the new 175 units are available.

Comparison shows that the café (and open-air swimming pool) have gone and been replaced by a modern housing estate. In the twilight of its career, Class 101 'Heritage' DMU No 101681 forms the 1450 Llandudno-Blaenau Ffestiniog service on 4 May 2000. *Gavin Morrison/JCH*

LLANDUDNO JUNCTION (Cyffordd Llandudno) (1): Following the closure of the loco shed in 1966, the carriage sheds were used as alternative accommodation. On 13 June 1981 there were four Class 25s, one Class 40 and a Class 120 DMU 'on shed'. As the years went by, the increased usage of DMUs, together with the loss of freight traffic, saw the requirements for locomotives greatly reduced, until the sheds were used only for the storage of out-of-service units.

On 2 July 1999 the building was still standing, although all tracks had been removed. Subsequently the site was completely cleared and a multi-screen cinema complex was to be built, as seen in the third picture taken on 28 March 2000. *All JCH*

LLANDUDNO JUNCTION (Cyffordd Llandudno) (2): Leaving the station with an up service on 22 June 1963 is ex-LMS 4-6-0 'Jubilee' Class No 45592 *Indore*. Llandudno Junction No 1 signal box, seen on the left, closed in 1968 and all the semaphore signals are long gone. As can be seen in the 'present' picture, there have also been a number of track modifications, and there is now no entry into the Junction station yard from the main line at the east end of the station. Class 101 'Heritage' DMU No 101677 has just left the station with the 1028 service from Llandudno to Blaenau Ffestiniog on 28 March 2000. *Gavin Morrison/JCH*

LLANDUDNO JUNCTION (Cyffordd Llandudno) (3): Ex-LNWR 0-8-0 '7F' No 49416 arrives at the Junction with an empty ballast train on 8 April 1958. Looking through the right-hand bridge arch, the line to Blaenau Ffestiniog can be seen going off into the Conwy Valley.

In the subsequent 42 years there have been some changes to the track configuration, but the view remains much as it was as Class 158 No 158759, in First North Western livery, passes the same spot on 4 May 2000. However, there has been considerable increase in the lineside greenery! *Gavin Morrison/JCH*

LLANDUDNO JUNCTION (Cyffordd Llandudno) (4): Only six years separate these two pictures, but a great deal has happened in between. On 28 January 1994 Nos 31304 and 31275 are propelling the nuclear flask from Trawsfynydd Power Station (at the end of the Blaenau Ffestiniog branch) into the yard. This will be joined by the flasks from Valley (ex-Wylfa Power Station) before being taken to Sellafield. Beyond the train, No 37422 is stabled and No 37503 can be seen at the head of a loaded ballast train from Penmaenmawr. The track off to the right leads to the old carriage sheds.

By 28 March 2000 the carriage sheds are being demolished to make way for a multi-screen cinema complex (see also pages 40-1) and the yard contains only a single Track Maintenance machine. Trawsfynydd Power Station has since closed and the empty flasks from Valley no longer use the yard. Note that the top of the station bridge tower has been changed. To the right of the station a Class 37 is leaving with a four coach up service. *Both JCH*

Mochdre to Rhyl

MOCHDRE is another place where the track alignment has been changed to accommodate the A55 Expressway. On 24 July 1982 Class 47 No 47174 is at the head of the 11-coach 0900 Euston-Bangor, passing the site of the old Mochdre & Pabo station, which closed in 1931. Preparation for the new positioning of the track is being carried out, and the A55 will eventually be built where the railway lines are. We can see how this was carried out in the 'present' photograph taken on 23 March 2000, showing Class 156 'Super Sprinter' No 156421 plus a two-car Class 158, forming the 1220 Crewe-Holyhead service. *Gavin Morrison/JCH*

COLWYN BAY (Bae Colwyn) (I): On 6 September 1961 ex-LMS Class '5' 4-6-0 No 45184 enters the station with the 8.10am Holyhead-Crewe train. At the time there were two 'island' platforms with four through lines, controlled by two signal boxes. The latter were replaced in 1968 by a single standard LMS design box, which was subsequently abolished in 1991.

The signal box remained standing until 2000, as there had been plans at one time for it to be used as an exhibit as part of a new tourist attraction, but the scheme did not materialise and the box was finally demolished. It can, however, be seen in the 'present' photograph behind Class 158 No 158756, forming the

49

COLWYN BAY (Bae Colwyn) (2): On the lovely late summer's day of 9 September 1961 'Black Five' 4-6-0 No 45438 is at the head of an up mixed freight, with Rhos-on-Sea and the Little Orme, near Llandudno, across the bay. The view has not changed, apart from the building of the A55 Expressway and a new bridge (the Tal-y-lan) over the road, seen in the bottom right-hand corner. Class 37 No 37415 heads the 1048 Holyhead-Birmingham New Street train on 23 March 2000. *I G Holt/ICH*

ABERGELE & PENSARN (Abergele a Phensarn) (1): For a short period in the 1980s, Class 33s, which had previously been mainly confined to the South of England, worked into North Wales. In this picture No 33040 is seen with the 1115 Crewe-Bangor service on 26 April 1986. At the time the station had two through lines and two platform roads, but in the 'present' shot, taken on 23 March 2000, it can be seen that the up through line has been removed. The station buildings on the down side are much the same, but on the up platform the one opposite the signal box has gone. The box remains open and some semaphore signals are still in place. Class 156 No 156427 (based at Newton Heath, Manchester) calls with the 1216 Manchester Piccadilly-Llandudno service. *Gavin Morrison/JCH*

ABERGELE & PENSARN (Abergele a Phensarn) (2): Class 40 No 40197 is ready to depart from the station on 14 August 1982 with the 0900 Llandudno-York 'holiday train'. There are several signal boxes on the North Wales coast line unusually located between the up and down lines. While some semaphores remain today, including the 'repeater' signal in front of the signal box, several have gone, including the two prominent in the 'past' picture, which would have been removed when the up through road was taken out. The white structure in the 'present' picture contains an axle-counter. On 21 January 2000, a Class 37 is at the head of the 1251 Holyhead-Crewe train. The locomotive and coaches were on hire to First North Western during the period following privatisation, when there was a great shortage of units. By the spring of 2000 the first of the new Class 175 'Coradia' units was on test, which would in time replace these remaining loco-hauled trains. *PDS/JCH*

RHYL (1): On Sunday 23 August 1959 BR Standard 4-6-0 No 75053 drifts past the Boating Lake at the west end of Rhyl, at the head of the 5.10pm Llandudno-Manchester Exchange train, with a consist of at least eight coaches; Exchange station closed in 1969. The four tracks suggest a period of much greater activity, but today the line is reduced to two tracks. On 25 October 1999 Class 37 No 37401 *Mary Queen of Scots* heads the 1251 Holyhead-Crewe service. Note the disappearance of the once 'ever-present' telegraph poles along the lineside. *Michael Mensing/JCH*

RHYL (2): When the 'past' picture was taken on 14 August 1982 the down platforms formed an 'island'. Nos 25153 and 25221 depart with the 0900 York/0857 Sheffield-Llandudno train – a summer Saturday holiday service. At the time Rhyl No 2 box was still open.

The 'present' picture, taken on 23 March 2000, shows that there is now only one up line, although on the down side there is both a 'platform' and a 'through' road. The station now has only two platforms, the bays having been removed. No 2 box was closed in 1990 but not demolished as it is a Grade 2 Listed building. Class 142 'Pacer' No 142030 is leaving the station with the 1316 Manchester Piccadilly-Llandudno service. *PDS/JCH*

Railway Station, Rhyl

RHYL (3): An interesting point in the undated photograph of the up platform (probably around the early 1900s) is that everyone is wearing a hat, varying from straw boaters and brown derbies to flat caps! The style of clothing certainly points to the early Edwardian period, *circa* 1904/5. A Vale of Clwyd train can just be seen in the bay on the left – the line to Denbigh survived for passengers until September 1955, and Denbigh MPD closed at the same time.

On 25 October 1999 the porter's truck has been replaced by a self-propelled trolley, but the main changes on the platform are the clear bilingual signs. The station building and forecourt underwent considerable refurbishment during 1994/5, but there is much that is the same between the two pictures. *Len's of Sutton/JCH*

Rhyl (4). Until the closure of Holyhead lost the Irish business, Freightliners were part of the everyday scene on the coast line, with regular services from London, Birmingham and Manchester. In the 'past' picture, taken on 14 August 1987, Class 47 No 47110 is passing under the fine gantry with 4H59, the Holyhead-Trafford Park service. To the left there is only rubble following the demolition of the carriage sheds.

Since then, the track configuration has been changed and the down 'through road' only commences just before the station. The two sidings on the left of the 'present' picture, taken on 19 June 1998, are primarily used by Engineer's vehicles. A few semaphore signals remain, operated from Rhyl No 1 signal box. Class 150 No 150419 forms the 0944 Llandudno-Manchester Piccadilly train. *Both JCH*

The Flintshire coast

GREENFIELD: With the third track of this once four-track main line still in position but rusty, Class 47 No 47454 passes Greenfield with the 1315 Holyhead-London Euston service on 18 February 1987. The locomotive carries the short-lived 'large logo' livery, while all but two of the coaches still carry BR blue and grey. The rapid growth of self-sown birch trees has all but obliterated the same view of the railway taken on 23 March 2000. The third track has gone, as have the Courtaulds factories, which were once rail-connected. *Both JCH*

HOLYWELL TOWN (Trefynnon): The 1¼-mile Holywell Town branch was opened by the LNWR as late as 1912, making it the last of the branches to stem from the Chester & Holyhead. It left the main line at Holywell Junction and climbed at a constant gradient of 1 in 27 towards the Town terminus. Ivatt '2MT' 2-6-2T No 41276 stands at the station with the usual single-coach 'motor train' on 28 June 1952. The journey from Holywell Town to Holywell Junction took just 8 minutes, including a stop at St Winifrides Halt.

Holywell Town closed to both passengers and goods in 1954, although a short stub from Holywell Junction continued to serve local industries until the mid-1960s. Since then part of the formation has been filled in and converted into a road and car park, while the station area itself has become a pleasant walkway. Little is recognisable in the 'present' picture, dated 5 May 2000, other than the line of the higher part of the ramp. *J. L. Darby, courtesy of E. N. Kneale/JCH*

FLINT (Fflint): Recalling the era of locomotive-hauled passenger trains on the trans-Pennine route, Class 45 'Peak' No 45122 passes Fflint with the 1115 Bangor-Newcastle service on 26 January 1985. Like many 'Peaks', No 45122 had been redeployed on secondary duties after being replaced on the Midland main line by InterCity 125 units.

The North Wales coast line became a honeypot for traditional locomotive-hauled passenger trains in the late 1990s as First North Western continued to operate three Class 37-hauled diagrams in addition to its DMU services. EWS-liveried Class 37/4 No 37401 *Mary Queen of Scots* passes through with the 1048 Holyhead-Birmingham New Street train on 27 July 1999. Fflint signal box was abolished in 1989 and the section was extended from Rockcliffe Hall to Holywell Junction. A new arrival is the giant sculpture of a human foot and ankle on the extreme left! *Both JCH*

CONNAH'S QUAY: A four-car Class 150 formation, with unit No 150138 leading, passes the already disused Rockcliffe Hall Power Station with the 1150 Llandudno-Crewe service on 18 February 1987. Twelve years later, on 27 July 1999, Class 158 unit No 158755 passes the same spot with the 1038 departure from Llandudno to Manchester Piccadilly. The railway itself has changed little, other than the removal of two semaphore signals, but the transformed skyline demonstrates the shift from coal-fired to gas-fired power generation, which led to the loss of so much rail-borne coal traffic in the 1990s. By a curious coincidence the new power station takes its gas from a processing plant at Point of Ayr, near the site of the colliery from which the old power station took its coal. *Both JC*

SANDYCROFT (1): Looking north-west on 27 July 1985, a Class 101 DMU passes the ex-LNWR signal box, dating back to 1900, with the 1400 Llandudno to Manchester Victoria service. The box is fringed to Mold Junction to the east and Rockcliffe Hall to the west. There was once a station here, but it closed in 1961.

The box is now open only as required, the track layout was simplified in 1986 by the removal of the down loop and, while some of the track is still in place, the up loop has also been abolished. Class 47 No 47822 heads the 0919 Holyhead to London Euston on 27 July 1999, exactly 14 years after the 'past' photograph. The Driving Brake Van will come into use at Crewe, when the diesel locomotive will be replaced by an electric locomotive at the rear of the train. *Both JCH*

SANDYCROFT (2): Nuclear flask traffic has been a familiar sight on the North Wales coast line since the opening of Trawsfynydd and Wylfa Power Stations in the 1960s. One loaded flask, flanked by barrier vans, is included in the consist of the daily Llandudno Junction-Warrington Arpley Speedlink working on 24 April 1985, headed by Class 25 No 25058. Other traffic includes aluminium from Holyhead, an empty oil tank from Holyhead, an empty cement tank from Bangor, and empty coal hoppers from Llandudno Junction, plus the obligatory brake van because the flask is classed as a dangerous load.

The haulage of nuclear flasks between various power stations and Sellafield was transferred to the BNFL subsidiary Direct Rail Services in 1999, bringing back the distinctive sight and sound of Class 20 locomotives to the North Wales coast. The weekly consignment of flasks from Wylfa, 7C40, the 1509 Valley-Carlisle, heads east near Sandycroft behind Nos 20312 and 20310 on 5 April 2000. None of the other traffic flows illustrated in the 1985 view is still carried by rail in 2000, although Llandudno Junction is still technically available for deliveries of household coal. *JCH/PDS*

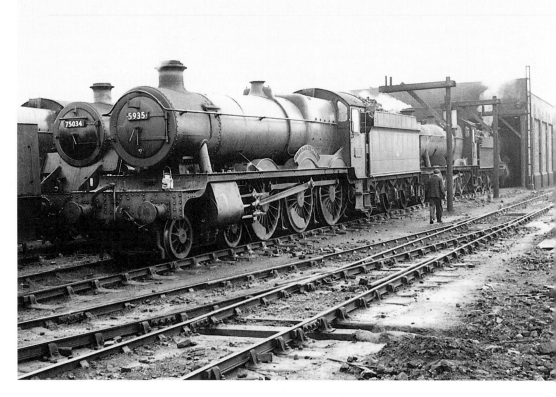

MOLD JUNCTION: The divergence of the Mold branch from the Chester to Holyhead main line was marked b the brick-built, dead-ended Mold Junction engine shed, coded 6B in BR days. GWR 'Hall' 4-6-0 No 5935 *Norto Hall* and BR standard '4MT' 4-6-0 No 75034 are among the locomotives stabled there on 22 October 196 Although Mold Junction was on LMS territory, GWR locomotives had become a common sight there since th closure of the former GWR depot in Chester in April 1960.

Mold Junction shed was closed in April 1966, but its shell has remained remarkably intact into the 21st century and the site around it is now occupied by a scrap dealer. The name Mold Junction survives in the signal box o the main line, not visible in this photograph. *Welsh Railways Research Circle, Stratton Collection/PDS*

Deeside and Chester

SEALAND: The former Great Central Railway route from Mickle Trafford to Dee Marsh Junction closed to passenger traffic in the 1960s and to freight in 1984. However, in 1986 it was re-opened as a single track with simplified signalling arrangements, mainly to carry three daily trainloads of hot-rolled steel coil from British Steel Ravenscraig to Shotton. A typical inbound service, 6M24, the 0525 Mossend to Dee Marsh Junction, passes Sealand on 17 October 1987 behind Class 20 locomotives Nos 20009 and 20154.

The closure of Ravenscraig left little traffic for the re-opened freight line, and it closed again in 1992, this time for good. Eight years later the trackbed was converted into a cycleway, with controversial plans by Cheshire and Flintshire County Councils to build a guided busway alongside. The 'present' view, dated 7 April 2000, shows the cycleway complete but not yet officially open. *Both PDS*

CHESTER SOUTH JUNCTION: Chester retained a fine selection of mechanical signal boxes and semaphore signals until the 1980s. A seven-car DMU, consisting mainly of Metropolitan-Cammell vehicles, passes Chester No 6 box en route to Llandudno on 15 July 1978. The tracks curving to the left form the third and least-used side of the triangle at Chester's west end, enabling traffic between the Wirral and North Wales to avoid Chester station and providing an easy reversing facility for loco-hauled trains. Stabled in a siding adjacent to the east side of the triangle is a Class 40 with Mark 1 stock, and just to the left of that is a Class 25 with empty oil tanks returning to Stanlow. The siding on the far right gives access to Chester wagon repair depot.

Chester was comprehensively re-signalled and rationalised in 1984. The overall amount of track was reduced, but most lines were signalled for bi-directional running to give greater operational flexibility, and the chord to the Hooton line was singled. Class 156 unit No 156429 recedes towards Chester station on 11 February 2000, forming the 1222 Bangor-Crewe service. The connection to Chester wagon repair depot had only recently been taken out of use when this photograph was taken. *Gavin Morrison/ICH*

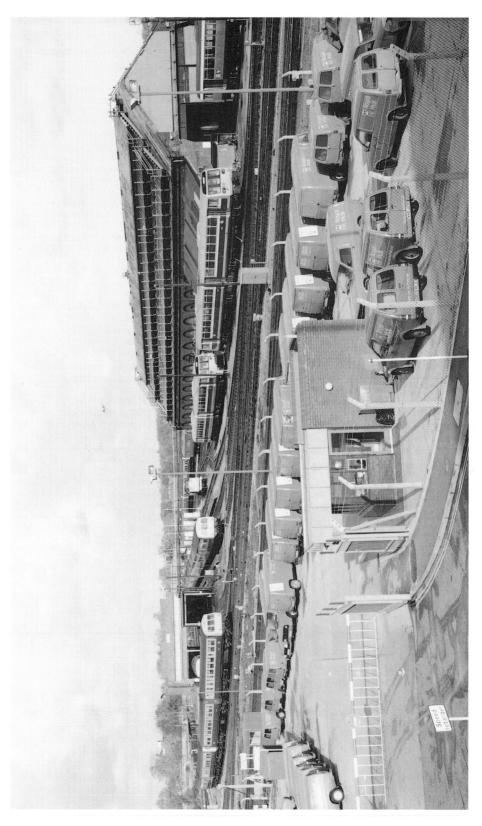

CHESTER DEPOT: In the 1980s and '90s Chester depot had no allocation of main-line locomotives, but was an important base for DMUs of both the first and second generations. This view of the depot dated 10 November 1985 shows a typical selection of Class 142 'Pacer' units and Class 101 Metropolitan-Cammell units, together with a lone Class 25 locomotive in the middle.

First North Western chose the existing depot site at Chester to build its new £17m maintenance facility for the Class 175 'Coradia' diesel multiple unit fleet. The new depot was completed in November 1999 and opened by the Lord Mayor of Chester. Unit No 175005 stands outside the depot on 19 June 2000, the day before revenue-earning services started. *JCH/PDS*

73

CHESTER EAST JUNCTION. The imposing Chester No 2 box, dating back to LNWR days and with a 182-lever frame, watches over the east end of Chester station as Class 47 No 47192 negotiates the freight lines with 6F25, the 1042 Bersham-Fiddlers Ferry coal train, on 13 August 1982. Chester freight depot, visible on the right, was still open for business but rarely handling any revenue-earning traffic.

The 1984 resignalling scheme brought a much simplified track layout; the freight avoiding lines on the north side of the station were reduced to a single bi-directional line with passing loops. A typical freight working of the modern era is 6F62, the 1232 Dee Marsh Junction to Warrington Arpley Enterprise working, pictured rejoining the main line on 5 May 2000 behind newly delivered Class 66 No 66191. Coal still passes through Chester but only in the opposite direction, destined mainly for Penyffordd cement works. *Both PDS*

75

ROSSETT: Although its passenger station closed as long ago as October 1964, Rossett remained a distinctive railway location with its GWR-style lower-quadrant semaphores until transformed by resignalling and rationalisation in the 1980s. A two-car Metropolitan-Cammell DMU recedes towards Wrexham on 8 June 1985 on an early morning service from Chester to Shrewsbury.

The singling of the Chester-Wrexham line was controversial and subject to delay, but it finally happened in 1986, at more or less the same time as the opening of the adjacent A483 trunk road. Rossett level crossing was closed to vehicular traffic as a cost-saving measure. Central Trains Class 158 No 158861 heads north at Rossett on 6 May 2000, forming the 0628 Wolverhampton-Chester service. *JCH/PDS*

Around Mold

LLONG was one of the smaller intermediate stations on the former LNWR route from Chester to Denbigh via Mold, and lost its passenger service in 1963. With the platforms now well grassed over, Class 25 No 25168 pauses to allow the guard to open the level crossing gates while working one of the occasional empty tank trains from Mold on 18 September 1980. Today, Llong station house is well preserved and the former level crossing gate is still in use, but the site of the Chester-bound platform has been cleared and a new shed encroaches on the trackbed. *Tom Heavyside/PDS*

the opening of the Mold-Denbigh stretch in 1869 until the axe fell in 1962. Standard Class '4' 4-6-0 No 75033 approaches Mold with the 5.00pm service from Denbigh to Chester on 28 April 1962, the last day of passenger operations on the line. Today the trackbed forms part of a supermarket car park, but the road overbridge on the left remains in place, as does the one from which both pictures were taken. *Michael Mensing/PDS*

MOLD (Yr Wyddgrug) (2): For nearly 20 years after the withdrawal of passenger services, the 4-mile stretch from Penyffordd to Mold remained in use for freight traffic, using a spur from the Wrexham-Bidston line at Penyfford. The last regular freight movements were tank traffic to the Synthite private siding at Mold, and one such train pictured passing the remains of Mold station on 18 September 1980, headed by Class 25 No 25168.

Although the costs of retaining the line to Mold had been pared to the minimum by converting all points to hand operation, the Synthite traffic was lost in the early 1980s and there was no other reason for keeping the line alive, so it was deleted from the BR Sectional Appendix in September 1984. Only the trees on the horizon serve to identify the location today. *Tom Heavyside/PDS*

COED TALON: One of Flintshire's more obscure railway junctions was Coed Talon, the focus of a substantial private system serving collieries and quarries in the Nercwys area. Coed Talon's first connection to the main-line railway system came in 1847 when the Chester & Holyhead Railway opened its branch from Ffrith Junction (on the Chester-Mold line, near Padeswood) to Llanfynydd. By the 1870s there was a second connection with the Chester-Mold line, from Coed Talon to Tryddyn Junction (just south of Mold), as well as a line heading south from Llanfynydd to Brymbo. The Ffrith Junction to Coed Talon stretch never carried passenger traffic and was closed completely in 1934. The remaining through route, from Mold via Coed Talon to Brymbo, was closed to passengers in 1950 and to goods in stages between 1951 and 1963. The photograph shows Fowler '4F' 0-6-0 No 44595 standing at Coed Talon station on 15 July 1963, just before the remaining stub from Mold to Coed Talon was abandoned.

After closure, the trackbed at the south end of Coed Talon station was swallowed up by a road-widening scheme, while part of the station yard became an extended car park for the Railway Inn. The wagon works, visible on the left-hand side of the 'past' picture, still stand today, but are obscured by a row of conifers. *H. C. Casserley/PDS*

The Wrexham area

GRESFORD: The Chester-Wrexham line was the most northerly outpost of the Great Western Railway and it retained its GWR atmosphere well into the BR era. '4300' Class 2-6-0 No 7310 pauses at Gresford station on Easter Monday, 18 April 1960, while working the 1.15pm local from Chester General to Wrexham General. The station had been de-staffed in 1955 and was closed in September 1962. Today no trace remains, and the site has been redeveloped for housing.

RHOSROBIN HALT: A reminder of the days when long-distance expresses used the now singled Chester-Wrexham line is provided by this view of ex-GWR 'County' Class 4-6-0 No 1017 *County of Hereford* passing the site of Rhosrobin Halt with the 2.35pm Birkenhead Woodside to London Paddington train on 18 April 1960. In the distance is Gresford Colliery, with several rakes of mineral wagons waiting in the BR exchange sidings.

The lean look of today's railway is epitomised by Class 158 unit No 158791 heading south with the 1128 Chester-Birmingham New Street service on 6 April 2000. The site of Gresford Colliery, which closed in 1973, is occupied by industrial and residential development. There appears to be enough space to re-instate the double track here, should Railtrack's aspirations attract suitable outside funding. *Michael Mensing/PDS*

GWERSYLLT: On Easter Monday, 18 April 1960, a newish two-car Derby 'Lightweight' DMU approaches Gwersyll
station with the 3.16pm New Brighton-Wrexham Central service. This line was the Great Central Railway's onl
entry into Wales, following its opening by the Wrexham, Mold & Connah's Quay Railway in 1886. The origina
name of the station was Gwersyllt & Wheatsheaf.

Little on the railway has changed here in nearly 40 years, apart from the usual sprouting of trees an
undergrowth. Class 153 No 153313 forms the 1432 from Bidston to Wrexham Central on 27 October 1999. *Michae
Mensing/JCH*

WREXHAM RHOS DDU: The Wrexham, Mold & Connah's Quay Railway built its own locomotive shed at Rhos Ddu, just north of Wrexham Exchange station on the west side of the line. The shed continued to provide a home for GCR and LNER traction until well into the BR era, providing a contrast with the GWR shed at Croes Newydd on the south side of the town. The closure of Rhos Ddu took place in January 1960, after which it was used as a store for withdrawn or unserviceable engines; the tracks are already weed-infested in this 1963 view. The site of Rhos Ddu shed is now occupied by a Remploy factory, pictured on 10 April 2000. *E. N. Kneale/PDS*

WREXHAM GENERAL (Cyffredinol Wrecsam): A busy moment on 25 June 1983, as Class 56 No 56082 heads towards Chester with empty BBA coil wagons and Class 47 No 47231 awaits the right of way with a loaded steel train bound for Shotton. At this time the two parallel routes heading north from Wrexham were still independently signalled, with two signal boxes facing each other across the tracks. Traffic on the Wrexham General-Chester line was controlled from the ex-GWR box on the right, partly hidden by the Class 56 locomotive, and traffic on the Wrexham Exchange-Bidston line was controlled by the ex-GCR box on the left.

The two signal boxes were closed in the late 1980s and control of the simplified track layout passed to Croes Newydd North Fork box. The Chester line is double-track through General station but reduces to single within a mile, while the Bidston line combines the two single tracks on the left of the picture into a double-track route. Class 156 No 156413 recedes towards Chester with the 1117 departure from Birmingham New Street on 27 October 1999. *Both JCH*

WREXHAM EXCHANGE (Cyfnewidfa Wrecsam): The Wrexham, Mold & Connah's Quay Railway managed to provide the best of both worlds for passengers to and from Wrexham: its Exchange station provided easy connection with the GWR at Wrexham General and its Central station was situated in the heart of the town. A steeply graded and curved line linked the two stations. Stanier 2-6-2T No 40131 climbs towards Exchange station with a northbound special excursion on 18 April 1960.

Undergrowth threatens to obscure the view of Class 153 unit No 153310 as it rounds the curve with an early morning Wrexham Central-Bidston service on 10 April 2000. The adjacent location of Exchange and General stations has finally been acknowledged and both are now known as Wrexham General. *Michael Mensing/PDS*

WREXHAM CENTRAL (Canolog Wrecsam): The 'basic railway' had already reached Wrexham Central when this view of Class 142 unit No 142046 was taken on 29 July 1987. In fact, the line had been reduced to a single dead-end 'siding' from Wrexham Exchange as long ago as the 1970s, after the last stretch of the former Cambrian Railways/GWR route towards Ellesmere was closed.

When is a closure not a closure? Wrexham Central station remains open today, used by the same hourly DMU service to and from Bidston as it was in 1987. But the platform was moved 350 metres towards Wrexham General in 1998 in order to allow redevelopment of the original town centre site. The only links between the 1987 picture and the 'present' one, taken in October 1999, are the tip of St Mary's cathedral spire on the right and a chimney stack in the left distance. *Both JCH*

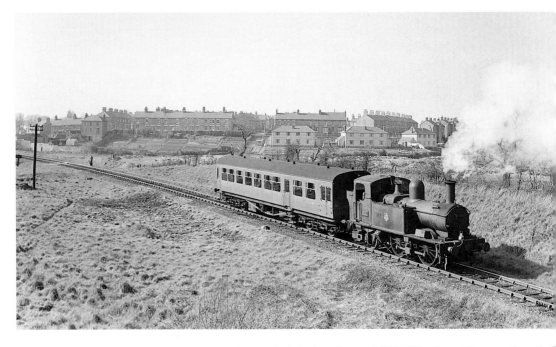

HIGHTOWN HALT: A typical scene at the urban end of the largely rural GWR Wrexham-Ellesmere branch i
provided by this view of '1400' Class 0-4-2T No 1438 leaving Hightown Halt with the 4.20pm departure from
Ellesmere on 18 April 1960. Passenger services between Wrexham and Ellesmere were withdrawn in Septembe
1962, while the last freight flow – to Abenbury on the outskirts of Wrexham – ceased in the 1970s. Cyclists and
pedestrians may use the formation today. *Michael Mensing/PDS*

WREXHAM WATERY ROAD: The concept of the railway-owned goods depot was still just about alive in the 1980s, although many depots were unstaffed and customers had to provide their own lifting and cartage. Wrexham Watery Road depot on 25 June 1985 was home to several ferry vans awaiting loading with steel products from Brymbo. In the run-round loop, meanwhile, is Class 47 No 47313 with the daily Speedlink trip working from Dee Marsh Junction to Warrington Arpley, conveying cement from Penyffordd as well as empty steel flats and loaded scrap wagons from British Steel Shotton.

BR's decision to pull out of wagonload freight sealed the fate of Watery Road depot, as it did with dozens of surviving station goods yards up and down the country, and an opportunity to sell the site for housing development was not to be missed. However, the run-round loop remains in use for various freight workings to and from the Bidston line, including the revitalised Enterprise wagonload service between Dee Marsh Junction and Warrington. Pictured in charge of the lunchtime departure from Dee Marsh Junction on 10 April 2000 is Class 37 No 37695, with three 'twin vans' conveying paper from Shotton to Irvine. All cement from Penyffordd is now conveyed by road, although coal is received there by rail. Most steel traffic to and from Shotton is conveyed by the three daily company trains to and from South Wales. *JCH/PDS*

CROES NEWYDD: The main wagon marshalling point for the Wrexham area was Croes Newydd yard, situated alongside the GWR Brymbo branch and reached by a triangular connection from the Wrexham-Ruabon line. In its final years Croes Newydd saw very little revenue-earning traffic, but the trackwork and signalling remained remarkably intact. Pulling away from the east end of the yard on 12 August 1982 is Class 25 No 25135 with a single GUV van in tow. This was a curious local shunt working from Wrexham General up side to Wrexham General down side, using the Croes Newydd triangle to avoid a run-round movement. The only other activity in the yard on that morning had been the tripping of some crippled wagons from Bersham Colliery.

Croes Newydd East and West signal boxes were taken out of use in 1983 and the yard was finally declared closed. A single track was retained alongside the yard to serve a new coal stocking site at the long-closed Gatewen Colliery, but this turned out to be short-lived and all traces of the railway were eventually removed. *Both PDS*

BRYMBO: An intricate network of industrial lines once served the steelworks and collieries around Brymbo. In later years all that remained was the former GWR branch from Croes Newydd, freight-only since the withdrawal of the Wrexham-Brymbo-Berwig passenger service in 1931. Brymbo steelworks still produced up to ten trains a day in each direction in the mid-1970s, carrying inward raw materials as well as outward finished product. Just leaving Brymbo on 12 July 1976 is Class 25 No 24063 with empty coal hoppers, coke hoppers and plate wagons for Croes Newydd. This was the last year of squadron service for the Class 24s.

During the late 1970s the various freight flows to and from Brymbo were progressively transferred to road. The branch handled its last revenue-earning traffic in October 1982, and its three signal boxes at Brymbo Middle, Brymbo East and Broughton Crossing were permanently secured out of use in February 1984. Brymbo steelworks itself closed in 1990. *Tom Heavyside/PDS*

BERSHAM: Class 25 No 5280 (later to become 25130) pushes a rake of empty 21-ton mineral wagons into Bersham Colliery sidings on 5 June 1972. Waiting to shunt the newly-arrived train is 1937-built *Hornet*, works number 1935. In the distance, just left of the signal box, is a short train of loaded wagons ready for departure.

Bersham Colliery closed in the mid-1980s in the aftermath of the year-long miners' strike, and the last trainloads of stockpiled coal left the yard in early 1987. The colliery itself, the last in the Wrexham area and one of only two in North Wales (the other was at Point of Ayr), was saved from demolition by becoming a museum. Class 156 unit No 156410 passes Bersham with the 1117 Birmingham New Street-Chester service on 30 June 1999.
Tom Heavyside/JCH

Ruabon to Dolgellau and Blaenau

LLANGOLLEN passenger station was built on a narrow, gently curving site on the banks of the River Dee; goods facilities were provided a short distance to the west. In March 1963 BR Standard No 75021 enters the station from the Ruabon direction.

Llangollen closed to passengers in 1965 and to freight in 1968. Within a month of final closure all track and signalling was removed, but this did not deter a group of determined enthusiasts from establishing a base there in 1975 with a view to re-opening the line. Today, thanks to the hard work and perseverance of the Llangollen Railway Society, the track extends 7½ miles from Llangollen to Carrog. It is, however, no longer possible to photograph a train arriving from the Ruabon direction because the tracks stop immediately under the road bridge. *E. N. Kneale/JCH*

GLYNDYFRDWY: Although the Ruabon to Dolgellau line formed the shortest route between North West England and many Welsh seaside resorts, it ran through a sparsely populated area west of Llangollen and most of it was single track. GWR '5700' Class 0-6-0PT No 4683 approaches Glyndyfrdwy with the 5.40pm Bala-Wrexham General local on 5 October 1963.

After more than 30 years of closure, the private Llangollen Railway extended its services over the Glyndyfrdwy-Carrog section in May 1996. Trains operate at weekends for most of the year, and daily from mid-April to the end of October. Providing an interesting contrast with the 'past' picture is Stanier 4-6-0 No 44806 with the 1050 departure from Carrog on **20 May 2000**. *Michael Mensing/PDS*

99

CORWEN: A railway junction was established at Corwen as early as 1865, when the GWR opened its route from Llangollen to link up with the recently opened LNWR Vale of Clwyd branch from Denbigh. The continuation westwards to Dolgellau was opened between 1866 and 1868. Entering Corwen station on 13 August 1953 is '4300' Class 2-6-0 No 6367 with the 3.45pm Ruabon to Barmouth train.

Closure of the Ruabon-Barmouth line was planned for January 1965, but the Llangollen-Bala Junction stretch succumbed one month earlier because of flood damage at Llanderfel. The station site today forms a trailer depot. The Llangollen Railway Society has set its sights on bringing trains back to Corwen, despite some trackbed encroachments at the Corwen end that will necessitate a diversion. *H. C. Casserley/PDS*

NANTCLWYD was one of the intermediate stations on the LNWR Vale of Clwyd (Rhyl-Ruthin-Corwen) line, illustrated here in the early years of the 20th century. The line was never more than a local route and fell into rapid decline after the Second World War. Passenger services between Ruthin and Corwen were withdrawn in 1953 and the line closed completely in 1962. No further use was found for the substantial station building at Nantclwyd and the whole area was cleared. *Len's of Sutton/PDS*

DOLGELLAU: The Cambrian and Great Western Railways formed an end-on junction at Dolgellau (spelt Dolgelly until the late 1890s and Dolgelley from then until 1960), allowing through running from Ruabon to the Cambrian Coast. The company distinction was lost when the Cambrian merged with the GWR in 1923 and Dolgellau became simply another intermediate station. Closure in 1965 was followed by a hasty demolition job, first by vandals, then by private contractors employed by BR. The station site is pictured on 11 January 1969, with track recovery about to start in earnest.

The site of the joint Cambrian/GWR station is now occupied by the A470 Dolgellau bypass, as recorded here on 25 September 1999. *By permission of the National Library of Wales, Geoff Charles collection/PDS*

PENMAENPOOL: The Cambrian opened a branch up the Mawddach estuary as far as Penmaenpool in the mid-1860s, later extended to Dolgellau to link up with GWR metals. Despite the small size of the village, Penmaenpool boasted a small engine shed that remained open until the line's closure in 1965. Passing Penmaenpool station in this late 1950s scene is a GWR '4300' Class 2-6-0 with a Barmouth-bound service.

Penmaenpool has been reluctant to forget its railway connections. Today people can enjoy a stroll along the former trackbed, pictured here on 21 May 2000. *E. N. Kneale/PDS*

ARENIG: Regarded by many as the wildest stretch of railway in England and Wales, the GWR line from Bala Junction to Blaenau Ffestiniog passed through lonely mountainous terrain, with a summit at Cwm Prysor some 1,200 feet above sea level. Arenig station, despite its remote location, was busy with quarry traffic and had sidings for 100 wagons. A pair of GWR '5700' Class 0-6-0PT locomotives, Nos 9793 and 9752, stand in the westbound platform with a well-laden mixed freight on 7 January 1961.

Passenger and freight services were withdrawn from Arenig in 1960 and 1961 respectively. The granite quarries have also closed and much of the former railway land has returned to nature. The line, with its impressive scenery, might have had a future as a tourist attraction, had it not been for the building of Llyn Celin reservoir over part of the trackbed. Planning powers were obtained for a diversion, but in the end the cost was considered prohibitive. *N. R. Knight/PDS*

TRAWSFYNYDD: This fine stage-managed photograph of Trawsfynydd station around the turn of the century serves to emphasise the labour-intensive nature of early railway operations. The locomotive is a '517' Class 0-4-2 tank.

Dated almost 100 years later, the 'present' photograph shows how the fortunes of the railway at Trawsfynydd subsequently rose and fell. During more prosperous times a second building was provided on the station platform, similar in style to the original. In 1961 the line was closed, and in 1968 the station building was converted into a private house. *By permission of the National Library of Wales, John Thomas collection/PDS*

MAENTWROG ROAD: Named rather ambitiously after the village several miles down the valley, Maentwrog Road station was one of the seven intermediate stations between Bala and Blaenau Ffestiniog. GWR '7400' Class 0-6-0PT No 7428 pauses at the single platform en route to Bala on 29 March 1959. Even ten years after Nationalisation the loco retains 'GWR' on its sides.

After its closure to passengers in 1961, the line from Blaenau Ffestiniog to just north of Trawsfynydd remained open for nuclear flask traffic from Trawsfynydd Power Station to Sellafield reprocessing plant. Regular flask traffic ceased in August 1995 following the closure of the power station, although there was also a one-off movement in April 1997. The line was declared closed in November 1998. Maentwrog Road station meanwhile is thriving in its residential role. *Gavin Morrison/ PDS*

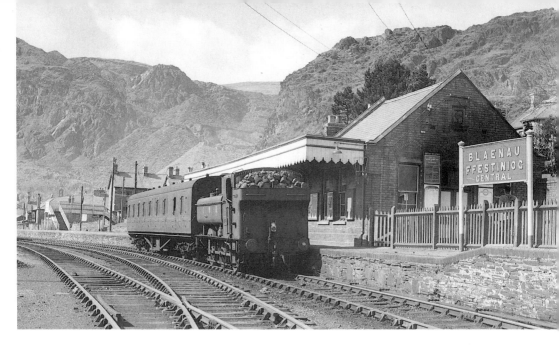

BLAENAU FFESTINIOG (1): The mountains of slate make this view of Blaenau Ffestiniog unmistakable, as No 7428 waits to leave with a Bala train on 30 March 1959. At this time there was still no physical connection between the GWR station and the LNWR one a short distance to the north, and any through passengers had to walk between the two.

After the closure of the Bala line, BR finally built a connection between the former LNWR and GWR metals in order to serve Trawsfynydd Power Station from the Llandudno Junction end. In 1982 the LNWR Blaenau Ffestiniog station was replaced by a new one on the former GWR site, also providing an interchange with the recently extended Ffestiniog Railway. Pictured in the station on 4 May 2000 is First North Western 'Heritage' Class 101 unit No 101677 waiting to form the 1145 to Llandudno. *Gavin Morrison/JCH*

BLAENAU FFESTINIOG (2): The narrow-gauge tracks of the Ffestiniog Railway dovetailed with the GWR's standard-gauge railway at the north end of Blaenau Ffestiniog Central station, as shown in this photograph, also dated 30 March 1959. Just visible in the station is No 7428 with its single-coach train to Bala.

Today, the realigned standard-gauge railway forms a through route from the north, used by the regular passenger service from Llandudno. The narrow-gauge tracks are completely separate, with new platforms for both lines connected by a footbridge. One of the Ffestiniog's 0-4-4-0T locomotives is leaving with the 1155 to Porthmadog on 4 May 2000. *Gavin Morrison/JCH*

Ruabon to Welshpool

RUABON (1): GWR '5800' Class 0-4-2T No 5810 approaches Ruabon station with the 3.45pm Wrexham General-Bala train on 9 August 1956. The shed plate on the smokebox door reads '84J', which was the Western Region code for Croes Newydd shed at that time.

The same view looking north from Ruabon today is devoid of any railway interest, although at least the double track line is well polished by freight and passenger trains, and there are no longer any plans to single it. *Brian Morrison/PDS*

RUABON (2): LNWR-designed 'G2' Class '7F' 0-8-0 No 49403 passes Ruabon with a mixed freight bound for Oxley on 9 August 1956. Ruabon at this time was still an important railway junction, with the former Cambrian Railways main line to Barmouth via Llangollen diverging from the GWR Shrewsbury route just south of the station.

Ruabon station was reduced to an unstaffed halt in 1974, and at the time of writing Central Trains provides a roughly two-hourly passenger service for most of the day. Class 158 unit No 158844 arrives with the 1128 Chester-Birmingham New Street on 27 October 1999. *Brian Morrison / ICH*

WESTON RHYN: Steam-age infrastructure persisted at Weston Rhyn, just south of Chirk, well into the era of 'Sprinter' units. One of the first generation of 'Sprinters', Class 150 No 150108, heads north with the 1403 Wolverhampton-Chester service on 26 September 1987. Close examination of the signals in the foreground reveals that one is lower quadrant and the other upper quadrant, a not unusual combination on former GWR lines that had been transferred to the London Midland Region.

Weston Rhyn lost its freight loops, crossover and semaphores as part of a local resignalling scheme. The level crossing is protected by automatic barriers and the nearest signal boxes are Gobowen to the south and Croes Newydd North Fork to the north. Class 158 unit No 158791 forms the 1516 Birmingham New Street-Chester service on 6 April 2000. *Both PDS*

OSWESTRY (1): Although Oswestry is not in Wales, it played an important part in the history of the Cambrian Railways company, which chose to locate its headquarters there, alongside the substantial locomotive and carriage works that it inherited from the Oswestry & Newtown Railway. On 28 August 1952 '2301' Class 0-6-0 No 2411 stands in Oswestry station with the 10.50am to Pwllheli, while 4-6-0 No 7819 *Hinton Manor* waits in the centre road.

The Cambrian main line via Oswestry closed as a through route in 1965 and the remaining passenger 'shuttle' between Gobowen and Oswestry was withdrawn in November 1966. General freight services at Oswestry were withdrawn in 1971, while ballast trains from Blodwel quarry continued to polish the single track through the station until 1988. This is the view in March 2000. *Brian Morrison/JCH*

117

OSWESTRY (2): Also on 28 August 1952, GWR '1400' Class 0-4-2T No 1473 stands in Oswestry station with the 10.35am auto train to Gobowen, where connections could be made with the main line between Chester and Shrewsbury. Much of Oswestry station was demolished shortly after closure, but the imposing Cambrian Railways building on the northbound platform survives to this day, albeit boarded up. The Cambrian Railways Society is still active in Oswestry and would like to see passenger trains running once again from the town. *Brian Morrison/JCH*

WELSHPOOL (Y Trallwng) (1): The people of Welshpool were disappointed when the Cambrian chose to locate its headquarters in Oswestry rather than Welshpool. Nevertheless, Welshpool was fortunate enough to be served by two main lines, the Cambrian route from Whitchurch to Aberystwyth and the LNWR/GWR joint line from Shrewsbury. Ex-GWR 'Manor' No 7803 *Barcote Manor* leaves Welshpool with the Paddington-bound 'Cambrian Coast Express' on 10 August 1956.

The commissioning of Radio Electronic Token Block signalling on former Cambrian lines heralded the closure of Welshpool box and most of the other signal boxes west of Shrewsbury. An even bigger change for Welshpool came with the building of the A483 bypass in 1992, forcing the railway to move to a new alignment. *Brian Morrison/JCH*

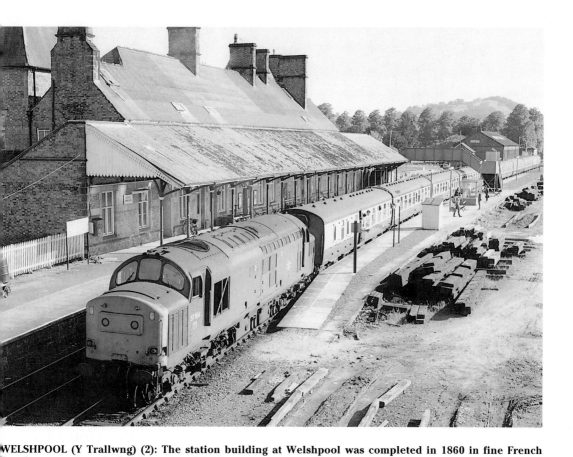

WELSHPOOL (Y Trallwng) (2): The station building at Welshpool was completed in 1860 in fine French Renaissance style as the headquarters of the Oswestry & Newtown Railway. It managed to survive the upheavals of Grouping and Nationalisation and forms an imposing backdrop to this view of Class 37 No 37164 with the 0753 Shrewsbury-Aberystwyth service on 10 June 1985.

Diversion of the railway to make way for the new A483 road has brought renewed prosperity to the O&N headquarters. A call at Welshpool's new island platform is made by a Central Trains Class 156 and Class 153 combination forming the 1129 Aberystwyth-Birmingham New Street service on 10 March 2000. *Both JCH*

Cambrian border branches

BLODWEL: The first few miles of the Tanat Valley Light Railway remained in regular use until the late 1980s, to serve a railway ballast loading point at Blodwel quarry. Class 25 No 25042 has just arrived at Blodwel on 21 August 1985 with 7J02, the 1012 empty ballast train from Bescot.

After the contract to move ballast from Blodwel ended in 1988, the branch was left intact for a possible inward flow of domestic waste. This, however, never came to fruition, and after 12 years of disuse some stretches of the line would need costly refettling – maybe even relaying – if ever a new freight opportunity were to occur. Little has changed meanwhile at the disused Blodwel loading terminal, pictured in March 2000. *Both PDS*

LLANRHAEADR MOCHNANT was one of ten intermediate stations on the Tanat Valley Light Railway from Oswestry to Llangynog. It became the terminus of the line after the upper section closed in 1952, with occasional goods workings persisting until 1960. A Stephenson Locomotive Society special visits the station on 20 September 1958, headed by Ivatt 'Mogul' 2-6-0 No 46509. The former station site is pictured again on 25 March 2000, with no railway traces evident. *H. C. Casserley/PDS*

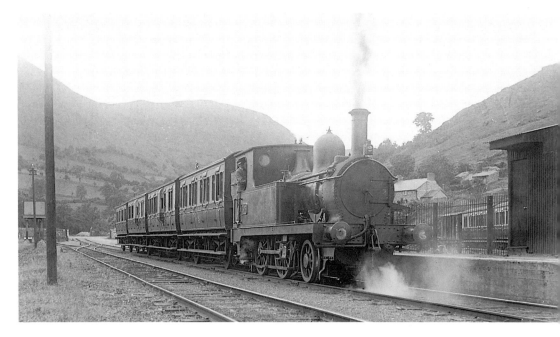

LLANGYNOG, the terminus of the line, nestled high up in the Tanat Valley, surrounded by the Berwyn Mountains. The line was built primarily to serve the lead and slate mines in the area, but also boasted an advertised passenger service from 1904 until 1951. The Tanat Valley Railway never thrived under independent management – it became insolvent almost upon its opening – and was taken over by the Cambrian Railways in 1921. This 1930s view of the terminus shows former Cambrian Railways 2-4-0T No 1196, one of three similar locomotives used on the line until the 1940s, heading a typical rake of four-wheeled carriages.

Llangynog station has become a peaceful caravan park in this remote corner of Wales. The railway has been gone for half a century, but one platform edge remains. *Len's of Sutton/PDS*

LLANFYLLIN (1): The Llanfyllin branch paralleled the Tanat Valley line as it threaded its way through pleasant border country from the Cambrian junction of Llanymynech. Unlike the Tanat Valley, the Llanfyllin branch was not a Light Railway but was built to main-line standards, enabling a wider range of traction and rolling-stock to be used. Pictured just after leaving Llanfyllin on 5 October 1963 is Ivatt 2-6-0 No 46512 with the 1.30pm to Oswestry.

Goods and passenger services were withdrawn from the Llanfyllin branch in 1964 and 1965 respectively. Parts of the trackbed are well preserved, as in this view dated 25 March 2000. *Michael Mensing/PDS*

LLANYMYNECH (2). With less than two years to go before closure, Llanymynech station is host to ıvatt 2-6-0 No 46512 with the 1.30pm departure to Oswestry on 5 October 1963. Today, the goods shed survives in commercial use, while the whole station area has been redeveloped with light industrial units. *Michael Mensing/PDS*

INDEX OF LOCATIONS

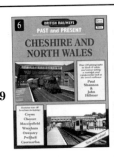